Beyond Gaming

How Virtual Reality Is Transforming Industries

Table of Contents

Chapter 1. Introduction

As we venture further into the digital era, the advancements in Virtual Reality technology are leading us far beyond the realms of gaming. In our Special Report, "Beyond Gaming: How Virtual Reality Is Transforming Industries," we delve into the fascinating ways in which VR is altering industries you may have never imagined. From immersive learning experiences in education to improved patient care in healthcare and even streamlining design processes in architecture, VR is truly reshaping our world. This report is a treasure trove of insights guaranteed to broaden your understanding of the evolving digital landscape. Don't miss out on exploring these revolutionary transformations – they could be the key your business needs to stay ahead in this era of technological upheaval. Let's step into the future together!

Chapter 2. Unveiling Virtual Reality: The Dawn of a New Era

Over the past few decades, technology has played an instrumental role in bringing remarkable transformations to our lives. Be it the breakthroughs of the internet, the impact of artificial intelligence, or the marvels of cloud computing, every advancement is proving that we are indeed living in an exciting digital age. And now, it is the turn of Virtual Reality (VR) to make its grand entrance onto this stage.

In its nascent phase, virtual reality was confined to the realm of science fiction, limited to animated simulations and video gaming. But as technology evolved, so did the potential applications of VR. Today, virtual reality is pushing boundaries in various sectors, revolutionizing the way we work, learn, and socialize.

2.1. The Idea of Virtual Reality

Long before the advent of modern VR technologies, the concept of simulating reality for educational, entertainment, or training purposes existed. From cave paintings to sophisticated flight simulators, humans have always attempted to mimic and display reality for various purposes. The term "Virtual Reality," however, was popularized in the late 1980s by Jaron Lanier, the founder of VPL Research.

Virtual reality can be defined as a computer-simulated environment that can be similar to or completely different from the real world. It immerses users in an interactive artificial environment, where they can interact with 3D world elements using electronic devices such as VR glasses or gloves fitted with sensors.

2.2. The Birth of VR Technologies

The groundwork for VR was laid down in the 1960s with the development of the first head-mounted display (HMD). Known as the "Telesphere Mask" and invented by Morton Heilig, this was the rudimentary beginnings of what we now know as VR headsets.

The momentum for VR grew stronger in the 1990s when tech companies started venturing into this field. Nintendo, a gaming giant, attempted to create a household VR gaming system named "Virtual Boy". However, due to technical limitations and high prices, it didn't find widespread acceptance.

Yet, the idea of VR persisted, and the real breakthrough came in 2010, with the invention of a prototype for the Oculus Rift by Palmer Luckey.

2.3. The Modern Age of VR: Oculus Rift and Beyond

Luckey's Oculus Rift was a watershed moment for the VR industry. The Rift offered a truly immersive VR experience with low latency and high frame rates, factors crucial for a convincing VR environment. This development attracted global tech giant Facebook's attention, who acquired Oculus in 2014.

Following the Oculus development, multiple tech heavyweights sought to stake their claim in the VR space. Valve Corporation collaborated with HTC to produce the popular Vive headset, while Sony launched their PlayStation VR system to considerable success.

In the meantime, Google introduced an affordable VR solution called Google Cardboard in 2014, lowering the entry barrier and making VR technology accessible for the masses.

2.4. Moving Beyond Gaming

Despite the initial focus on gaming, VR has found many applications outside the entertainment realm. From education to medicine, from architecture to the automobile industry, the use cases for VR are practically unlimited.

In architecture, for instance, VR has made it possible to create walk-through simulations of buildings before they are built, providing architects with a tool to spot potential design flaws. In education, immersive VR experiences can help students understand complex theories and concepts more easily.

In the healthcare field, VR has shown tremendous potential in medical training, therapy, and patient care. It allows surgeons to simulate surgeries for training purposes, offers therapeutic relief for patients with chronic pain, and aids in treating various phobias.

While still in the early stages of development and application, the future of VR presents fabulous opportunities for innovation and growth across different sectors.

2.5. The Future of VR

As the technology improves and becomes more affordable, VR's transformative potential will continue to increase. The tech world expects a future where VR will go beyond sight and sound and incorporate other senses such as touch and smell.

The next few years could see VR being utilized in numerous novel ways. We may experience virtual shopping, where customers can 'try on' clothes or 'visit' the store from the comfort of their homes. Traditional video conferencing could be replaced by VR meetings, making remote work more engaging than ever before.

In the realm of education, we could see more extensive uses of VR, ranging from virtual tours of historical locations to accurate simulations of scientific phenomena.

In healthcare, VR could be used to provide empathy training for doctors, simulate complex surgical procedures for training, or offer detailed patient visualization for diagnostics.

However, transitioning into this world reimagined by VR doesn't come without challenges. Questions regarding data privacy, potential health issues, and the digital divide are topics of on-going concern and discussion.

In conclusion, the rise of VR technology heralds a new era in the digital landscape. An era where virtual is the new reality. An era where VR holds the power to transform how we perceive and interact with the world. With the dawn breaking on this new epoch, the next few chapters of the VR story are yet to unfold. Yet, one thing is sure: the VR revolution is here, and it's here to change our world in ways that we have yet to wholly comprehend.

Chapter 3. Beyond Gaming: Exploring New Realms

Years ago, the world was introduced to Virtual Reality (VR) with promise of immersive gaming experiences. Its evolution, however, has been remarkable, transcending the confines of the gaming industry and changing the paradigm across numerous sectors. We now stand at the vortex of a technological maelstrom that promises to overturn conventional wisdom and unlock potentials scarcely considered. Perhaps, as we delve deeper into the digital landscape, we must learn to see virtual reality not just as a tool, but as a new reality that offers endless possibilities and opportunities: a limitless dimension shaping a new future.

3.1. Education: The Birth of Virtual Classrooms

VR has the potential to entirely recalibrate the way educational content is delivered. Imagine a world where students are no longer confined within four walls or limited by geographical boundaries. Instead of reading about the Great Wall of China, they traverse the ancient stones; rather than hearing about the wonders of the deep sea, they experience it in all its awe-inspiring glory. Medical students might perform complex procedures in controlled simulations, mitigating risk while augmenting learning. By transforming abstract concepts into tangible experiences, VR paves the way for a more immersive, dynamic, and impactful method of delivering education.

3.2. Medicine and Healthcare: Revolutionizing Patient Care

The rippling influence of VR in healthcare is no less profound. Surgeons are now harnessing the power of this technology to perform complex operations more accurately and safely. VR allows a surgeon to visualize the patient's anatomy in a detailed 3D image, enabling them to make critical decisions with unprecedented precision.

Moreover, VR can significantly enhance the therapeutic process for patients. Utilizing VR for exposure therapy, for instance, has shown great promise for patients with phobias or post-traumatic stress disorder (PTSD). This form of treatment places individuals in a controlled virtual environment where they can confront and learn to manage their fears.

3.3. Architecture and Design: Shaping the Structures of Tomorrow

In the world of architecture and design, VR is changing the game. Architects are now free to construct intricate models in a virtual setting, saving valuable time and resources compared to traditional prototyping methods. Clients can take a virtual tour of their future homes or offices before a single brick is laid. This not only provides a tangible representation of the final product for better understanding, but also highlights potential flaws or improvements much earlier in the design process.

3.4. Retail and E-commerce: Crafting Immersive Experiences

The retail industry is embracing VR with open arms, especially in the e-commerce sphere where tactile interactions are lacking. Virtual showrooms facilitate an immersive browsing experience akin to brick-and-mortar stores, allowing customers to inspect items virtually. Moreover, personalized VR experiences can foster a deeper connection with customers and fortify their brand loyalty.

3.5. Manufacturing: Enhancing Product Development and Training

Manufacturing companies can leverage VR to create realistic prototypes and streamline the product development process. VR allows all stakeholders to view, manipulate, and modify a 3D model of the product before actual manufacturing, reducing errors and improving efficiency.

In addition, VR can significantly improve the safety and effectiveness of worker training. Instead of following instructions in a training manual, employees can dive into a virtual environment that emulates real-life conditions – from operating complex heavy machinery to dealing with hazardous situations.

3.6. Future Outlook: The Dawn of a New Era

While VR's impact is quite discernable in the sectors discussed above, it's important to note that we're still in the early stages of what this technology can offer. Industries yet untouched await the transformative power of VR, while even the gaming arena, where VR found its initial footing, continues to evolve and refine the immersive experience.

Virtual reality has the potential to transcend geographical barriers, reinvent learning, transform viewer experiences, refine surgical procedures, redefine property tours, and so much more. And as it does, businesses must continually adapt to stay ahead in this era of technological upheaval.

Indeed, as we collectively stride towards the future, the value of exploring and embracing these new digital realms cannot be overstated. If we open our minds to the possibilities, who knows what kind of future we might shape or what inspirational realities we might create – a concept that is no longer virtual but a tangible new world, indeed a new reality.

Chapter 4. Virtual Reality and Education: The Next Generation Learning

There has been a seismic shift in the way education is being delivered and perceived - driven by the rise of digital technologies. Virtual Reality (VR) technology, with its unique ability to offer immersive experiences and facilitate active learning, is at the vanguard of this revolution, offering educators and students a new world of possibilities. In this chapter, we delve deep into the intersection of education and VR, exploring the ways VR is not just enhancing, but redefining teaching and learning paradigms. We believe this exploration will provide actionable insights and stir thoughtful conversations on charting the future course of the edutech space.

4.1. Understanding VR in Education

At its core, VR is about immersion, presenting users with a computer-generated simulation of a three-dimensional environment that can be explored and interacted with. In the educational context, this takes the form of virtual classrooms, laboratories, or field trips, where students can learn through observation, experimentation, and direct interaction with the virtual material.

The application of VR in education is not about replacing traditional teaching methods, but complementing them. It's about building an enhanced pedagogical model that leverages the strengths of both physical and digital experiences. Traditional classrooms are essential for direct interactions, fostering social-emotional learning and building relationships. On the other hand, virtual classrooms underscore the importance of experiential learning, bringing abstract concepts to life, and taking students to places and times that would otherwise be impossible.

4.2. The Promise and Potential of VR in Education

The first, and most obvious benefit of VR in education, is that it makes learning more engaging. According to a study by the University of Maryland, students remember information better when it is presented in a virtual environment, as compared to a desktop computer. This points to the potential for VR to facilitate deeper understanding and improve retention.

VR's immersive nature allows students to learn by doing. The practice can lead to higher rates of understanding, retention, and application of the concepts learned, as opposed to passive listening. Further, VR can cut through the limitations of physical space, resources, or safety concerns. Labs, field trips, or even historical events can be recreated within a virtual world, enabling students to experience them without leaving the classroom.

If we take a step back and look at the broader picture, VR has the potential to democratize education. By enabling remote learning, VR can offer educational opportunities to students in rural or conflict-affected areas, ensuring that learning does not come to a standstill due to geographical or political challenges.

4.3. Practical Applications of VR in Education

There are numerous examples of how VR is being practicality used in the education sector:

1. Virtual field trips: Google has developed 'Expeditions' - an application that allows students to explore landmarks, dive

underwater, or visit outer space. By expanding the concept of a field trip beyond the constraints of geography, students can gain a truly global perspective.

2. STEM Education: VR has a pivotal role to play in teaching science, technology, engineering, and math (STEM) subjects by transforming abstract, complex concepts into tangible, interactive models. For instance, medical students can carry out virtual dissections or visualize molecular structures in three dimensions.

3. Skill training: VR can offer immersive simulations for real-world scenarios, enabling students to practice and hone their skills. For instance, teacher training programs can create simulations of classroom situations, thus giving teachers an opportunity to gain hands-on experience and practice their approach.

4.4. The Way Forward

While the potential of VR in education is immense, there are challenges to be overcome. High costs of VR gear and the lack of VR-ready content are prominent barriers. There are also concerns about the effect of prolonged VR use on mental and physical health, privacy issues, and the digital divide.

Yet, the narrative around VR in education is largely positive, propelled by continuous advancements in technology, dropping prices of VR equipment, and an increasing recognition of VR's educational benefits. As the edutech landscape evolves, we are moving towards a future where VR is a standard tool in education - as ubiquitous as the textbook. It promises a world of education where learning is more about experiences than mere information consumption, where students are explorers and creators, not just consumers.

To unlock the full potential of VR in education, we need to undertake concerted efforts involving teachers, policymakers, technologists, and researchers. The road might be paved with challenges, but the prizes at the end—enhanced learning, improved outcomes, equitable access to education—are worth it.

Chapter 5. The Virtual Therapist: Transforming Health and Therapy

Advancements in technologies such as Virtual Reality (VR) have triggered a significant transformation across various sectors. The healthcare industry is one such realm where VR holds immense potential, ranging from improving patient outcomes to bringing a new dimension to mental health therapy.

5.1. The Advent of Virtual Reality in Healthcare

VR's introduction to healthcare might seem recent, but it dates back to the 1990s, when researchers began dabbling in it as a therapeutic tool. Early examples included simple applications such as Needle Phobia VR, which aided children overcome their fear of injections by providing a distraction.

However, the real turning point was the launch of Oculus Rift in 2012, which drastically brought down the cost of consumer VR hardware. Factoring in the maturity of supporting technologies such as high-speed internet and high-density data storage, this was the perfect time for VR technologies to make a mark in the healthcare industry.

5.2. VR as a Therapeutic Tool

Fast forward to today, VR is increasingly employed as a significant part of pain management, cognitive therapy, physical therapy, and mental health therapy. Each of these domains utilizes VR's immersive capacity to create controlled environments where patients can safely manage distressing symptoms, learn new coping strategies, and ultimately, improve their quality of life.

In pain management, for instance, immersive VR experiences can distract patients from painful procedures or chronic discomfort. A study conducted by Brennan Spiegel, MD out of Cedars-Sinai hospital, demonstrated a significant reduction in pain scores for patients using VR, as compared to a control group.

5.3. VR-based Exposure Therapy

For mental health, one of the most significant methods employed is VR Exposure Therapy (VRET). By simulating situations that cause anxiety or distress, therapists can help patients confront and manage their fears in a safe and controlled manner.

VRET offers several benefits over traditional exposure therapy. Firstly, the controlled environment minimizes any associated risk while allowing the therapist to customize the degree of exposure. Secondly, it brings therapy within reach for patients who might not have access to real-life exposures. Lastly, VRET's immersive nature offers an overall better therapeutic and patient engagement compared to classical exposure therapy.

5.4. Intricacies of Developing VR Therapy Applications

A significant aspect of VR therapy's success depends on the depth and realism of the VR environment. Minimizing sensory discrepancies between the real world and the virtual environment is crucial. Otherwise, it could lead to breaks in presence, adversely affecting the therapy outcomes.

The process begins with identifying the target user group and understanding their needs. For instance, a VR application designed for aging adults coping with memory decline would prioritize simplicity, ease of use, and gentle haptic feedback, while one targeting PTSD in war veterans might focus on recreating battlefield stimuli.

Once these parameters are laid out, the VR environment is designed and developed accordingly. The design phase usually involves a mix of subject experts, UX/UI designers, and technology experts working together to ensure a perfect blend of realism, efficiency, and user-friendliness.

5.5. Evaluating the Effectiveness of VR Therapies

Measuring the effectiveness of VR therapies is essential to their acceptance and adoption. Quantitative data collected from VR applications includes duration, frequency, and progress reports on various therapy parameters, which can be analyzed for efficacy.

Additionally, physiological data such as heart rate, galvanic skin response, and respiration rate can offer objective insight into the patient's responses, providing valuable feedback for therapy adjustments. Patient feedback and qualitative interviews add a crucial layer of subjective understanding of a patient's experience, supplementing the objective data.

5.6. Challenges and Prospects

Despite its considerable potential, wide-scale adoption of VR in therapy is still an uphill task. Major challenges include the affordability of VR gear and the required computational power, ensuring the privacy and security of patient data, and potential side effects like motion sickness.

However, the future of VR in therapy shines bright. As technology continues to advance and these challenges are tackled, the potential of a VR integrated healthcare system offers a tantalizing glimpse into the future – a future where technology and human care merge to deliver the best possible healthcare outcomes.

Overall, the integration of VR into healthcare and therapy is not merely a gimmick. It is, indeed, an evidence-based advancement that offers a myriad of possibilities to improve patient outcomes, provide unprecedented therapeutic tools, and revolutionize the healthcare landscape. With continuous research and advancing technology, the promise of VR therapy grows stronger every day.

Chapter 6. VR in Architecture: Building the Future Virtually

The advent of Virtual Reality (VR) in architecture revolutionizes how architects think, design, and interact with their projects, reshaping the landscape of the industry. The immersive quality of VR creates a whole new approach to architectural design and collaborative processes. It's a tool that integrates abstract concepts and tangible reality in a manner that old sketching methods or even current CAD and BIM technologies never could.

6.1. The Confluence of Architecture and Virtual Reality

Virtual Reality has initiated a new era in the realm of architectural design. Previously, architects and clients had to rely on 2D drawings and physical models to communicate design intent. But these traditional methods often fail to convey spatial relationships and user-experience, especially complex, intricate designs.

The ability of VR to recreate a life-like environment and provide users with a sensory vividness previously unmatchable introduces a paradigm shift in how we understand and interpret space. With VR, architects can explore their designs in an immersive three-dimensional space, allowing them to experience their creations as closely to reality as possible. Clients can also navigate through space, providing immediate, relevant feedback, reducing potential misunderstandings and the costs that come with redesign.

6.2. The Design Process: Drawing in Space

In the design phase, sketching and drawing serve as essential tools to architects. From preliminary hand-drawn sketches to detailed 3D models on software, these are sequential steps in the development of an architectural design. VR elevates this process by enabling architects to draw and design in a 3D virtual space.

Software such as Tilt Brush, SketchUp VR, and others allow architects to immerse themselves in their design, sketching in the same 3D space they are creating. They can draw a line in the air and walk around it, visualizing it from all dimensions. This interaction offers a perspective that could lead to innovative design solutions, as well as faster recognition and remedy of potential design problems.

6.3. walkthroughs and Client Presentations

Presenting an architectural design to a client can be challenging. The disparity between the architect's vision and the client's understanding can lead to miscommunications. Physical models or 2D/3D digital renderings have their limits in showcasing a realistic sense of space.

With VR, clients are offered a full-immersive walkthrough of the design. They can experience space, size, proportions, materiality, and even lighting conditions. This engagement with the proposed structure ignites an understanding of the design intent that goes beyond technical specifications. Clients are also able to provide real-time feedback for architects to make appropriate changes and adjustments.

6.4. Virtual Collaboration: Team-working in Virtual 3D Space

Collaborative work in architectural firms often involves team members huddled around shared tables, discussing 2D plans or 3D models. Today, with distributed teams becoming more common, VR offers a virtual collaboration environment where remote team members can simultaneously investigate a 3D virtual model, irrespective of their physical locations. Real-time editing and communication during such sessions enhance productivity and streamline decision-making.

6.5. The Future: VR and Sustainable Design

Environmental sustainability is a pivotal aspect of contemporary architecture. Embedding energy-efficient building systems and achieving minimal environmental impact are prevalent in architectural practices. VR is poised to aid this movement by simulating a building's environmental impacts such as lighting, airflow, heat consumption, and water management in its design stage. This predictive analysis can guide critical decisions, leading to more sustainable building techniques and materials.

VR in architecture, although in its earlier stage, is truly representing the future of the industry. Its immersive, interactive, and transformative nature is redefining how architects design, collaborate, present, and envisage structures.

However, like every new technology, it does present challenges. These include high initial costs, software maturity, technical proficiency required to handle VR technology, and the inevitable resistance to change from traditional practices. But these hurdles are outweighed by the prospects of productivity, efficiency, better collaborative experiences, and a more in-depth understanding and exploration of architectural design.

In conclusion, as we step into a future where technology increasingly infiltrates every aspect of our lives, VR's role in architecture becomes not just a fanciful speculation, but an inevitable reality. It is essential for professionals to understand and leverage this technology to enhance design processes, client-interactions, and the realization of more innovative, sustainable structures. The virtual door to the future of architecture is wide open, and it promises an exciting journey.

Chapter 7. Step into the Screen: Virtual Reality and Entertainment

Virtual Reality (VR) has indeed proven to be a game-changer for the entertainment industry. Its immersive nature promises a level of involvement and connection to stories and characters that was hitherto unimaginable. VR's potential lies not just in the creation of a whole new form of narrative media but in its capacity to fundamentally change the way we perceive entertainment. It is a transformation that is revolutionizing the core of storytelling, visualization, and the overall entertainment experience.

7.1. A New Narrative Spectrum

In traditional forms of media such as film or television, the narrative arc unfolds from the perspective of an external observer; we view the world through a chosen lens regardless of the level of emotional connection or investment in the storyline. However, Virtual Reality breaks open these traditional boundaries and allows the user to step inside the narrative, providing the user with a first-person perspective that makes the narrative their own.

Being enveloped by a created world provides a surreal sense of immersion. The narrative does not merely unfold before the viewers; they are part of its creation. It is almost as if the narrative was sculpted around the viewer, who is at the heart of the experience rather than on the sidelines. This revolutionizes perceptions, promising not just passive absorption but active involvement.

7.2. The Power of Presence

Being present within a narrative is an incredibly powerful and affecting experience. VR uses a multitude of devices to trick our senses into believing that we are in a different world, a place constructed by the narrative. The sense of presence is what separates VR from other visual media. It's not just about seeing a new world; it's about being in that world.

7.3. Reinventing Visualization

Virtual reality is not just about reshaping narrative or even the sense of presence. It's also transforming the way we visualize material. VR pushes the boundaries of cinematic frameworks, shattering the limitations of a 16:9 frame. Cinematography is now about exploring 360-degree immersive environments. Directors need to rethink everything from shot compositions to narratives built around a moving, responsive viewer.

7.4. The Joy of Interactive Entertainment

One of the most profound effects of VR on the entertainment industry has been its capacity for interactive entertainment. VR lets the audience directly interact with the environment or narrative. Video games using VR technology have gained enormous popularity. The ability to interact and alter the course of a storyline on the fly creates profound engagement and makes gaming extraordinarily immersive.

Simultaneously, VR allows game designers to craft landscapes, build worlds, and synthesize atmospheres like never before. This degree of unrivaled customization carries the potential to create immensely personal and unique experiences for each player.

7.5. Pushing the Boundaries of Art and Performance

Virtual Reality offers the same disruptive capacity in the cultural spheres. The potential of this immersive technology in performance art and installations is massive. It facilitates artists to construct landscapes, shape immersive installations, and weave narratives that blur the line between the real and the virtual. These virtual spaces can augment or replace physical interaction, opening a world of possibilities for art and culture's future.

7.6. The Future Beckons

The potential of VR is infinite; its capabilities are only limited to the bounds of the human imagination. The rate of technological advancements and steadily decreasing costs will see VR technology grow more accessible to consumers, propelling its impact even further.

As we teeter on the edge of a digital era where reality can be built and manipulated, the entertainment industry has a responsibility to harness this exciting technology ethically and creatively. By understanding and respecting Virtual Reality's transformational potential, we open doors to a new dimension promising rich and immersive experiences that are not just consumed but lived.

This new norm in entertainment is brimming with challenges and opportunities. Embracing the VR world in its entirety requires us to adjourn our old projections about entertainment and reevaluate its potential in the light of Virtual Reality.

The integration of VR in our entertainment compass aligns us with a future where stories don't merely belong in books or on screens; they belong around us, waiting to be lived and experienced in their immersive glory. A future where we do not just see or hear stories, but we inhabit them, stepping through the looking glass into a reality of our design. Just like Alice in Wonderland, each step we take can lead us towards unimaginable reality, rich with myriad experiences yet to unfold.

Chapter 8. Revitalizing Retail: The VR Shopping Experience

The world of retail has been significantly shaped by digital trends over the past decade, and Virtual Reality (VR) stands out among the most indulging digital phenomena in the retail sector today. VR bridges the gap between the virtual and physical store experiences, bestowing shoppers with the capability to navigate through a digitally replicated store, a feat that sitting at home and scrolling on a 2D screen can't achieve.

8.1. The Concept

VR finds an avenue where conventional digital retail leaves off. The essence of VR shopping lies in giving consumers the traditional store 'feel' from anywhere, anytime. An immersive 360-degree view enables shoppers to walk down aisles, pick up products, inspect them, and even try them on in certain cases.

The leverage VR provides is twofold. Firstly, it adds a new dimension to online shopping, creating moments of joy and discovery, akin to in-store shopping. Secondly, it offers informative and personalized shopping experiences tailored to each user's needs and preferences, supplementing the comfort of online shopping.

8.2. Creating Immersive Shopping Experiences

E-retailers have been quick to grasp the potential of VR in transforming the shopping experience. Some have delivered real-time, three-dimensional shopping environments that replicate in-store shopping right down to product layouts and signage. In these virtual stores, shoppers can view products from multiple angles, learn more about product features, and even try on items like clothes or eyewear before making a purchase.

Virtual reality also allows retailers to create themed or situational shopping scenarios, like furnishing an empty room or pairing a shirt with trousers. These scenarios provide a platform for consumers to experiment with products outside the bounds of physical constraints, essentially allowing them to 'try before they buy' in a virtual world.

8.3. Personalization and Data Capabilities of VR

VR takes personalization to an unprecedented level. It facilitates the collection of intricate behavioral data, such as dwell time, head movements, and browsing patterns. These metrics offer a new depth of understanding into consumer preferences, enabling retailers to better predict buying behavior and customize the shopping experience accordingly.

Moreover, VR's capability to customize spaces based on user behavior and preferences creates an individually curated shopping experience. This means a personalized shopping environment based on shopping habits, a potential game-changer in email campaigns or customer loyalty programs.

8.4. The VR Dressing Room

One area where VR truly shines in retail is the fitting room experience. Some of the frontrunners in the fashion industry have integrated VR into their platforms to enable users to try on clothes virtually. This solves a significant pain point of online shopping - the inability to try before you buy - leading to reduced returns and increased customer satisfaction.

Customers can see how clothes fit, display different sizes and colors, and even get style recommendations based on the items in their virtual shopping cart. This experience brings them a step closer to buying the garment with confidence, mirroring the assurance they get in physical stores.

8.5. Bridging Physical and Digital Retail

VR shopping is not just confined to e-commerce; it has already started transforming physical retail spaces. Retailers are experimenting with VR to mix physical and virtual experiences. For example, interactive VR booths in stores can take customers on a virtual tour of the product catalog, allowing them to try products in various combinations or environments before making a purchase decision.

This blend of physical and digital experiences is giving rise to 'Phygital' retail, a concept that combines the best elements of online and offline shopping experiences. Here, VR serves as the suitable in-between, stretching the possibilities of retail in both domains.

8.6. VR and The Future of Retail

There's no doubt that the coming years will witness more profound implications of VR in the retail sector. As VR equipment becomes more cost-effective and its user base grows, VR's retail potential will be increasingly tapped. Moving forward, VR will spark a retail revolution where shopping extends beyond a mere transaction and becomes more of a personalized, interactive activity. Retailers who are geared for this change will undoubtedly be in a favorable position to engage consumers and retain their loyalty in this rapidly evolving retail landscape.

Virtual reality is more than just a developing trend in retail. It has the potential to rejuvenate the retail industry, offering a fresh, personalized, and engaging pathway to reach consumers. As we adapt to a world increasingly straddling the physical and digital domains, VR is sure to emerge as a major player in defining the retail industry's future. The VR shopping experience is transforming, and we are at the exciting cusp of this newfound digital reality.

Chapter 9. Immersive Journalism: A New Era of Storytelling

In the age of social media, information sharing has become instantaneous. News and current events transcend geographical boundaries in mere seconds. In this digital era, innovations like Virtual Reality (VR) are paving the way for immersive journalism, offering a fresh, more engaging approach to storytelling.

VR technology offers unique experiences by immersing the user in a life-like virtual environment, stimulating their senses in a way that traditional media cannot. This immersive aspect allows consumers to "experience" news stories firsthand instead of simply reading or hearing about them.

9.1. The Concept and Evolution of Immersive Journalism

Immersive Journalism is a technique that leverages VR, AR (Augmented Reality), and MR (Mixed Reality) to give the audience a first-hand experience of the story being told. The concept was first coined and introduced by Nonny de la Peña, known as 'the godmother of VR', during the Sundance Film Festival in 2012 with her project 'Hunger in Los Angeles'.

Over the years, this concept has evolved beyond initial experimentation. Reputationally-respected news outlets such as The New York Times, BBC, and The Guardian have recognized immersive journalism's potential and are adopting VR technology to create compelling news features that offer a first-person perspective. These experiences place the viewer in the reporter's shoes, enabling an empathetic understanding that mere text or linear video cannot convey.

9.2. Advantages of Immersive Journalism

One of the significant advantages of immersive journalism is the ability to generate empathy. VR technology transports the viewers into the story, making them witnesses rather than passive consumers. This kind of immersion generates a sense of empathy and emotional connection that typical print and broadcast journalism struggles to provide.

VR can also resurrect historical events, making history tangible. For example, the BBC's interactive VR experience "1943 Berlin Blitz" puts viewers in the shoes of a war correspondent during a bomber flight over Berlin during World War II. This not only makes history accessible but also relatable, making significant historical lessons resonate effectively.

9.3. The Application of VR in Immersive Journalism

There are various ways to apply VR in immersive journalism. One of the simplest is VR photographic journalism, using 360-degree photos to deliver a visceral, real-world experience for viewers. A more complex application involves combining VR with computer-generated imagery (CGI) for a hyperreal experience. VR documentaries, VR live news, and VR investigative journalism are also formats being explored by different news organizations globally.

Moreover, journalism can leverage VR's interactive capacity, presenting news as participative scenarios where the audience can freely explore environments and objects related to the report. All these applications aim to engage viewers on a deeper level, steering clear of the abstract, and moving towards experiential storytelling.

9.4. Challenges Facing Immersive Journalism

While VR presents numerous opportunities for immersive journalism, it does not come without challenges. Producing VR content requires new skills and technology beyond conventional journalism capabilities, leading to higher production costs. There are ethical and editorial considerations, too, particularly around the risk of distorting reality or making experiences so visceral that they distress or harm viewers.

Further, VR adoption amongst consumers is still a hurdle. Despite steady growth, VR's use is not yet commonplace. However, as technology advancements make VR headsets more affordable, immersive journalism is expected to gain more traction.

9.5. The Future: Pioneering a New Dimension of Journalism

The potential of immersive journalism is vast, painting a promising future. As technology continues to advance, we can expect more sophisticated VR experiences that will continue to redefine the way news is consumed. By capitalizing on immersive technology, journalism can achieve a closer connection to its audience, deepening understanding and nurturing empathy.

In the end, VR is not intended to replace traditional journalism; instead, it is another tool in the storyteller's kit, a medium that promises to engage and inform audiences in unparalleled ways. With the clear potential to improve the journalistic landscape, VR will undoubtedly play a vital role as the industry continues to evolve.

Even while facing challenges, immersive journalism represents an exciting new era of storytelling, one that brings the world closer together, even as we venture further into the digital age.

Creating authentic, engaging stories that foster connection, encourage empathy, and provide access to unique experiences is now more than an aspiration – thanks to technology, it's an ever-evolving reality. As we continue exploring the potential of technology in journalism, VR offers a glimpse of a future where news is more than just information – it is an experience.

Chapter 10. Sustainable Futures: Virtual Reality in Environmental Conservation

The intersection of Virtual Reality (VR) and environmental conservation is a topic of great significance today, yielding compelling and effective tools for resource management, ecological awareness, and environmental education. Through the lenses of VR, humans can interact with ecosystems and biological processes that they otherwise couldn't. With the distinctive power to create immersive experiences, this technology promises prospective transformative shifts in our dealings with the environment.

10.1. The Emergence of VR in Nature Preservation

Virtual Reality has surfaced as a pivotal disruptor within the field of nature preservation. Traditional conservation efforts are certainly important; however, their practical execution often meets obstacles, such as accessibility to remote locations or real-time replication of environmental conditions. VR overcomes these challenges by creating digital simulacrum of threatened habitats, permitting scientists, policymakers, and the public to virtually explore endangered ecosystems from anywhere in the world. For instance, Sansar's "The Apollo Museum and Nature Trek" allows users to explore the biodiversity of Brazilian Amazon virtually.

Being a medium of 3D visualization, VR can also enhance the understanding and communication of spatial data. Scientists can use VR solutions to visualize correlations and patterns in environmental data collected by satellites and drones, thereby aiding in targeted conservation efforts.

10.2. VR and Climate Change Education

The issue of environmental conservation is often abstract to the public because its effects are not always directly observable or locally witnessed. VR can bridge this understanding gap by providing realistic simulations of climate change impacts, stimulating an emotional response strong enough to drive behavioral changes.

Projects like "The Crystal Reef," a VR film and game developed by Stanford University's Virtual Human Interaction Lab, leverages VR to provide the users an immersive experience of ocean acidification. Likewise, "Tree" a VR exhibition, lets you experience the life-cycle of a rainforest tree, from a seed growing in the underside to its ultimate demise due to deforestation. These experiences employ the power of VR to communicate the urgency of climate change in a visceral, impacting way that traditional methods fail to achieve.

10.3. Enhancing Environmental Research

The use of VR in environmental research includes resource management, biodiversity identification, and behavioral studies. Scientists and ecologists can utilize VR to simulate environmental changes and predict their impact, or to document complex ecosystems for further study.

For instance, the Australian Research Centre for Human Evolution used VR to capture a 500,000-year-old coral reef in Indonesia, allowing the direct comparison of reef environments over time. This type of virtual exploration not only allows for historical analysis but can showcase potential future outcomes under different ecological conditions.

10.4. VR in Green Design and Planning

Green architecture and urban planning have been fundamental in constructing sustainable societies. Incorporation of VR in this field can enhance decision-making processes by producing detailed, immersive models of bio-based designs. Visually realistic simulations help to evaluate the efficacy of green designs before physical construction, therefore expediting the trial-and-error process.

Virtual reality is becoming a vital tool for 'green' architects and designers, given its capacity to visually represent the environmental impact of a proposed structure or layout. It conveniently brings forth the minutest details, which can be instrumental in making green design adjustments that can make a project more environmentally friendly and sustainable.

10.5. The Future of VR in Environmental Conservation

As VR technology continues to advance, so too will the reach and impact of its applications in environmental conservation. Researchers will possess greater ability to monitor and map out earth's most endangered ecosystems, and individuals around the world will be able to engage more personally with the places and wildlife they're working to protect. From viewing the world from a tree's perspective to exploring the depths of the most fragile coral reefs, VR offers powerful tools to foster awareness, empathy, and action among users, thereby becoming a great catalyst for environmental stewardship.

As we step into the future, the union of VR and environmental conservation can pioneer a more engaged, informed and empathetic society, encouraging us all to cherish, protect, and sustainably interact with our natural world.

Chapter 11. Final Thoughts: The Promise and Perils of a Virtual World

The wild growth and adoption of virtual reality (VR) are nothing short of remarkable. It's no longer just about immersive experiences in gaming. It's seeping into different facets of our lives, revolutionizing the way we learn, work, and live. However, as we head forward into the world of virtual reality, we must also be aware of the pitfalls and challenges that could potentially shadow its promises.

11.1. Understanding the Promise

The promise of virtual reality is vast and sweeping, beginning with its ability to bring vivid, high-quality experiences to anyone, anywhere. Whether it's students taking virtual tours of the International Space Station, architects visualizing the buildings they're designing, or patients being able to practice mobility skills in safe, controlled environments, VR stands to revolutionize many sectors of our societies.

The immersive nature of VR blurs the boundaries between the physical and digital spheres, enabling experiences that are not just viewed, but profoundly felt. This emotional impact can prove invaluable in several fields. In education, for instance, VR can provide experiential learning, making education more engaging and memorable.

In business, VR can offer new methods for collaboration and communal learning. It allows remote teams to interact as though they are in the same room, creating an unprecedented level of collaboration that physical distances once hindered. In the medical field, VR provides an immersive platform for training, preparing health professionals for real-world scenarios in safe, simulated environments.

The promise of VR extends even into entertainment and media. Gone are the days when the consumer was only a passive viewer. Through VR, consumers can engage with content in ways never before possible. They become active participants in their entertainment, and media creators gain a new narrative tool.

11.2. Recognizing the Perils

Despite the vast potential of virtual reality, there are perils to the technology that should not go overlooked. Notably, as with any emerging technology, the ethical implications are significant and complex.

One of the first challenges is the potential for addiction. With VR's immersive experiences becoming increasingly compelling, there might be a risk of users finding their virtual life more appealing than their physical one. While this could be merely a concern for some, it could potentially lead to a form of digital addiction for others.

Privacy issues represent another significant concern. As VR systems can track users' every move and reaction, serious consideration needs to be given to how this data is stored, used, and secured. Without stringent regulation and control, there are fears that sensitive personal data might end up in the hands of ill-intentioned parties.

Furthermore, there's a risk of widening the digital divide. As VR technology continues to advance and requires more sophisticated – and expensive – equipment, there's a risk that those with fewer resources may be left behind. This divide can result in increased inequity, particularly if VR becomes a dominant mode of communication or interaction in certain sectors.

In addition, there's the question of health risks. Some users experience physical discomfort such as nausea or dizziness while using VR, a condition known as "cybersickness." Also, extended use of VR headsets may have detrimental effects on eyesight and posture.

11.3. Entering a Balanced Future

The rise of virtual reality offers a world full of promise and potential, paired with new perils and challenges. It's critical for businesses, governments, and individuals alike to understand both in order to move forward responsibly.

Those exploring VR's potential should consider forging a balanced approach, one that maximizes the benefits while minimizing the drawbacks. New frameworks need to be developed to guide VR's use, from regulatory measures protecting privacy to design principles prioritizing user wellbeing. Furthermore, steps are required to ensure VR technology is not only accessible and affordable but used in a manner that promotes inclusivity and equality.

If we are to fully embrace virtual reality, we must see it for what it truly is: a powerful tool, capable of tremendous good, that holds as much promise as it does peril. It's up to us to decide how this tool will be used and managed, how we navigate its challenges, and how ultimately, we permit it to transform our reality.